WOMEN IN HISTORY

MODERN WORLD

FIONA MACDONALD

Chrysalis Children's Books

This edition published in 2003 by
Chrysalis Children's Books
The Chrysalis Building, Bramley Rd, London W10 6SP

ISBN 1 84138 888 2

British Library Cataloguing in Publication Data for this book is available from the British Library.

Series editor: Claire Edwards
Editor: Angela Royston
Series designer: Jamie Asher
Designer: Zoe Quayle
Cover Designer: Keren-Orr Greenfeld
Picture researcher: Diana Morris
Consultant: Ann Dingsdale

Printed in Hong Kong
10 9 8 7 6 5 4 3 2 1

Picture acknowledgements:
AFP/Corbis: 13b, 25t, 33b.
Bettmann/Corbis: f cover bl, b cover l, b cover tr, 3r, 1b, 4b, 5l, 6b, 7t, 7b, 9t, 9c, 10bl, 10c, 12l, 12b, 14b, 15t, 16br, 18bl, 18tr, 19bl, 19tr, 20c, 20b, 22tr, 27br, 34tr, 35t, 37b, 38cl, 41b, 43t.
Jacques M Chenet/Corbis: 22b, 31t, 43br.
© Judy Chicago 1979, Photo © Donald Woodman: 21t.
Dean Conger/Corbis: 24b.
Corbis: 30b.
Rufus F Folkks/Corbis: 45bl.
Owen Franken/Corbis: 3cl, 17t, 31, 40bl.

Ronald Grant :13t.
Hulton-Deutsch Collection/Corbis: 3l, 5br, 8b, 20bl, 25bl, 26b, 29t, 29b, 32b, 33t, 34bl, 42bl, 42tr.
James Marshall/Corbis: 41t.
Stephanie Maze/Corbis: 28b.
Jack Moebes/Corbis: 11b.
PA News PL: 44bl.
Raissa Page/Format: 36b, 45cr.
Reprinted by permission of the Peters Fraser & Dunlop Group Ltd: 23t.
Max Rankin: 40tl.
Roger Ressmeyer/Corbis: f cover cl, 3c, 31b, 39t.
Renato Rotolo/Corbis: f cover br, 45cl.
Moshe Shai/Corbis: 38br.
Leif Skoogfors/Corbis: 3cr, 36tr.
Bradley Smith/Corbis: 15tc.
Paula Solloway/Format: 27t.
Ted Streshinsky/Corbis: 16c.
Peter Turnley/Corbis: 35br.

CONTENTS

World war's end

From 1939 to 1945, Europe, the USA and many other nations fought the Second World War. By the time peace was declared in 1945 millions of men's and women's lives had been changed for ever.

> When all the men came back after the war the bank said, 'Thank you very much for doing all the work for our men while they've been away... Now you've got to teach the men...' We went back to ... the shorthand and the typing...
>
> BANK WORKER FROM NORTHERN ENGLAND, INTERVIEWED AROUND 1950

Coping alone

The war brought heartbreak and loneliness to many women. Their husbands or boyfriends were killed or badly wounded. Some couples found it hard to live apart, and their marriages ended in divorce. Many women and children in countries that had been bombed had to leave their homes and live in miserable conditions as refugees.

Home at last! An American family are reunited after the Second World War. Many families were not so lucky.

Not enough food

For those who survived, there was a shortage of food and fuel throughout Europe. Even in America, which was a rich country, mothers found it difficult to feed families on the small rations of food that they were allowed.

A queue of 5000 unemployed men waits outside government offices in New York City, in about 1948. The US government created special jobs for returning soldiers.

Jobs for the boys

In 1945, when American women war-workers were interviewed, four-fifths of them said they would like to continue working, even though the war was over. That was not what men in Europe or the USA hoped to hear. When the war ended, governments – and many ordinary men – demanded that women leave work and go back home. Otherwise soldiers, sailors and airmen returning from the war would be unemployed.

Changing roles

In wartime, men fighting in the armed forces often thought of the women and children they had left behind. It gave them courage to know that they were fighting to save their families. But when men returned from war, they found that their wives and sisters had changed. Wartime work had made them bolder and more confident. They were used to being independent and were less likely to do what men told them. Men were no longer sure of what to expect from women.

Women's war work

Women did not fight in battles in the war, but they played an important part just the same. They kept shops, offices, buses, trains and newspapers running while men were away. They worked in factories, making guns, tanks and planes. Women proved they could do dirty and dangerous work just as well as men. And they had even enjoyed it.

Customers hand over ration coupons so that they can buy bread in a London store, 1946. Food was rationed in Europe and America during the war, and in Europe for several years afterwards.

The Cold War

The years from 1945 until 1989 are known as the Cold War. At that time two rival groups of nations were enemies. The USSR and its allies in Eastern Europe were communists. The USA and its allies around the world were capitalists. Each set of beliefs had advantages and disadvantages for women.

> It is for woman as mother ... to restore security to our insecure world.
>
> AGNES E MEYER, JOURNALIST
> ATLANTIC MONTHLY, 1950

Men's equals

Under communist law, women were treated as men's equals. It was easy for women to work because education and child care were free. But in return, women were expected to behave like men. They did the same jobs as men, and they could not stay at home with their children unless the state allowed them to. Like men, they had little freedom because the state controlled their lives.

Unable to fit in

Some women who lived in communist countries enjoyed the opportunity to work. Others found it hard to behave like a man. Communist laws gave women equality, but women were not promoted to top jobs at work or in the government. And anyone who criticized the government was sent to prison or disappeared (this often meant that they had been executed without a trial).

Men's helpers

In capitalist countries at the start of the Cold War, women were not equal to men, either in law or in everyday life. They were regarded as men's helpers and sometimes as men's property. With few laws to protect them, they had to rely on their husbands or families. Divorce was not easy, and married women were expected to stay at home as housewives.

In the 1950s, advertisements and magazines showed women how the ideal housewife should look and act. This picture shows a young woman, glamorously dressed, preparing a meal for her family.

Women marching through Washington DC, the capital of the USA, to protest against nuclear weapons. Many people feared that the Cold War might become a nuclear war.

Imprisoned in the home?

In capitalist countries, some women enjoyed their lives as housewives. Others wanted the freedom to choose their own way of life. It was almost impossible for women to have a proper career as well as look after a family.

Witch-hunts

During the late 1940s and early 1950s, any American who dared to criticize the government was accused of supporting communism. Women were especially affected by these witch-hunts. Because they were brought up and educated children, as mothers and teachers, women were expected to have correct (non-communist) views. Even the most innocent remarks were treated with suspicion. For example, in 1947, film star Ginger Rogers was accused of being a communist, because she read out these lines from a Hollywood filmscript: 'share and share alike – that's real democracy'.

ETHEL ROSENBERG

Ethel Rosenberg (1915–1953) was born in New York. Even as a young woman, she had left-wing views and her husband, Julius, was a member of the communist party. By 1950, anyone with left-wing views was suspected of being a friend of the USSR and a potential spy. Ethel's brother, David Greenglass, worked for the US government, developing nuclear weapons. He claimed that Ethel and Julius asked him to pass secret information to the USSR. Ethel and Julius insisted that they were innocent. Public hatred increased when people learned that Ethel and Julius were Jewish (many Americans were prejudiced against Jews at that time). Ethel and Julius Rosenberg were put to death in 1953 – the only Americans ever executed for treason in peacetime. Today, many historians think they were unjustly killed.

Ethel and Julius Rosenberg

Civil rights

According to the US Constitution, black men and women in America had equal voting rights with whites. But in many states, segregation (forcing black and white people to live apart) was still common. Many black people were prevented from voting by local white people. From the early 1950s black women, some of them young girls, campaigned against segregation and for full civil rights.

Racist university

In 1956, a black student, Autherine Lucy, tried to enter classes at the University of Alabama. But after white students chanted racist slogans and threw rotten eggs at her, Lucy was expelled from the University.

Students' sit-in

In 1960, four black college students in North Carolina held a protest. They occupied a segregated snack bar. Other black and white students organized protests too, often led by women. For example, in 1960 black teenager Ruby Smith protested by using whites-only lavatories. She willingly went to prison to gain publicity for civil rights demands.

Segregated schools

Often black and white children were not allowed to go to the same state schools, and the schools for black children were often not very good. In 1954 a black father took the local education service to court, after his daughter, Linda Brown (aged 8), was not allowed to attend her nearest school. He won his case.

Black women and men drinking ice cream sodas at a soda-fountain (snack bar). Before civil rights protests, almost all places open to the public in the south of the USA were segregated.

The National Guard protect black students from attack by white people who want the school to continue as a whites-only school.

New respect, new skills

Civil rights were not just a women's struggle, as the women who took part in marches and boycotts were keen to point out. They wanted freedom and justice for all people – men, women and children. But by taking part in protests, women campaigners gained new confidence and learned new skills. They also won great respect.

Suffering for freedom

Throughout the 1960s, civil rights protesters were often attacked. For example, in 1963 Mississippi farm-worker Fanny Lou Hamer was arrested on her way home from a civil rights meeting. She was badly beaten by the police. In Selma, Alabama, after a day of mass protest marches for civil rights in 1965, Viola Liuzzo, a civil rights worker, was driving a car with black passengers. She was chased at high speed by white extremists in another car and shot dead.

ROSA PARKS

Rosa Parks (born 1913) has been called the Mother of the Civil Rights Movement. She was born in Montgomery, Alabama, USA. Black people living there – and in many other southern cities – could not use the same schools, shops, hospitals or even churches as whites. In 1955, she refused to give up her seat on a bus to a white man, even though the local bus company demanded that she should. For a year after her action, black people boycotted all the buses in Montgomery.

Rosa Parks being interviewed by news reporters on her way to stand trial. The bus boycott she began was the start of mass protests for civil rights throughout the USA.

1954	The US Supreme Court decides segregation (separate facilities such as schools and hospitals for people of different ethnic origins) is unlawful.
1963	Protests leader Martin Luther King makes his famous 'I have a dream...' speech.
1964	A Civil Rights Act bans racial discrimination in employment, and in all public places.
1968	A Civil Rights Act is extended to ban discrimination in housing and property.
1968	Martin Luther King is assassinated.

WOMEN AT HOME

An ideal family

The idea that women's place was in the home was a very old one. Women had fought against it for more than 100 years. Now, in 1945, it was becoming fashionable again. Why did so many women accept it?

> Husbands are like fires. They go out when unattended.
>
> ZsaZsa Gabor,
> Actress, 1960

Patriotic duty

In the late 1940s and 1950s, political leaders and others told women that it was their duty to provide a home for returning war heroes, and to produce children to rebuild the postwar world.

Wifely support

According to this view, a man's career needed a woman's support. Husbands worked hard and brought home money from the outside world of work. Wives helped them by cooking their meals, cleaning the house and ironing their shirts. They also entertained their boss with tact and charm. There was no time for a woman to have her own career.

The suburban dream. An American couple and their three young children return home from an outing in their car. Many poor Americans hoped to achieve a lifestyle like this one day.

In the 1950s, women at home were encouraged to develop feminine skills, such as flower-arranging and knitting.

No hope alone

There were also practical reasons why women gave up their wartime independence and accepted going back to being housewives. Women's wages were still much lower than men's, even in well-trained, professional jobs. It was hard for a woman to support herself alone, and almost impossible for her to support her children. Social life was organized around families. Single women, however successful, had lower social status than wives.

Catch your man!

In 1950s in Europe and America, single women did not have a full place in society. More than 90 per cent of women were married at least once in their lives. Girls were worried that they might fail to catch a husband. Even young women with a university education hoped to marry soon after they were 21 years old.

Baby boom

After the war, as soldiers returned home to their wives, many babies were born. In America in 1946, there were more than half a million more births than in the year before. The baby boom peaked in 1957, with a record 4.3 million births in the USA. Large families were fashionable – most American women wanted at least four children. But they limited women's freedom. Only women who could afford to pay someone to look after their children could have a career too.

BOOKS FOR GIRLS AND BOYS

In the 1950s, books and comics for children carried the same message as books and films for adults. Men and women were not equal. Children's books showed boys and girls with very different interests and skills. Boys were strong, brave and adventurous. Girls were often timid and easily scared. When things went wrong, they were likely to burst into tears. Writers assumed that girls would only be interested in clothes, ballet, ponies and stories about groups of school-friends, and that boys would only want to read about soldiers, explorers, sport and big machines.

Women with wealthy husbands bought fashionable clothes and expensive toys for their children. Their lives were comfortable, but many were bored.

Changing images

During the war, women wore trousers, overalls and flat shoes, just like men. After the war, designers created a new, feminine image for women. It was closely linked to other changes in women's lives.

In the 1950s dresses had tight waists and full-skirts and were worn with the latest stiletto (spike-heeled) shoes. This black silk cocktail dress (for early evening parties) was designed in 1955.

Glamour

What did these female film stars look like? Film-star fashions can be summed up in two words – womanly and glamorous. Fashionable women were expected to have rounded figures. After years of wartime shortages, when many women had gone hungry, thinness was not admired.

Natural curves?

People thought that a curvy shape was a sign that a woman could bear children. It also made it very clear that women were not the same as men. These ideas fitted in with the belief that a woman's role was to raise a family, not compete with men at work. Even so, the ideal shape was not a natural one, but was created to fit in with fashion. To achieve this shape, many women wore uncomfortable padded bras and tight girdles.

Film idols

Films were the most popular form of entertainment in the late 1940s and 1950s. Film stars were as well known as television personalities are today. Women copied the stars' clothes, make-up and hair styles. Men pinned up photos of female stars in factories and workshops. Magazines related gossip and scandal about the stars' lives.

American film star Doris Day (born 1924) was admired for her plump, healthy good looks. She was said to look like a typical girl-next-door.

Marilyn Monroe (1926–1962) was a talented actress and film star. But she was most famous for her curvy figure, revealing dresses, bleached blonde hair and dramatic make-up.

Red lips and high heels

Fashionable women liked to copy Marilyn Monroe, the most glamorous film star of all. They wore heavy, dramatic make-up and bleached their hair, though this was still rather shocking. High, stiletto heels were first sold in 1955. They were popular, and soon became symbols of smartness and sex appeal, though they were often painful to wear, and made running impossible. But film-star glamour was carefully controlled. For example, in 1952, the men who ran US television companies introduced strict rules about dress for women workers. They said that all women who appeared on television should only wear clothes with a high neckline.

BARBIE

Barbie dolls were first sold in 1959, by Californian businesswoman Ruth Handler. Barbie was not like other dolls, but was more adult-looking. Her shape was, and still is, very unnatural. Her chest is too big, her waist too small, and her legs too long. Until recently, her tiny feet were always on tiptoe so she could wear high heels.

Does this matter? Some people think so. More than one billion Barbie dolls have been sold in 140 countries. Some people suggest that Barbie sends out dangerous messages to girls about how they should look, and makes them unhappy that they cannot match Barbie's appearance. People also wonder whether Barbie's figure has encouraged young women to develop eating disorders, or to have dangerous cosmetic surgery to change their shape.

Ruth Handler proudly displays a special edition doll, created for Barbie's fortieth anniversary celebrations in 1999.

What's wrong?

During the 1960s, many women who had rushed eagerly into marriage began to feel dissatisfied. Some also felt they had failed. Their husbands expected them to match the image of the ideal housewife shown in the media and they could not do it. Doctors reported large numbers of women seeking help for depression. Other women developed eating disorders or drank too much alcohol. What was their problem?

> The problem which has no name ... is simply the fact that American women are kept from growing to their full human capacities ...
>
> BETTY FRIEDAN, AUTHOR OF *THE FEMININE MYSTIQUE*, 1963

Feminine mystique

In 1963, an American writer called Betty Friedan published a book called *The Feminine Mystique*. (Mystique means mystery.) In the book she wrote that during the 1950s, women had been tricked into accepting a view of how women should be. But this view had been invented by men. It was not reasonable, she wrote, to expect every woman to find their fulfilment as a wife and as a mother. Not all women were born with some magical, in-built talent to be home-makers or to care for men and children.

Trapped at home

The problem for many women was that they were trapped at home, and were not free to be themselves. Women would find life more interesting if they went out to work, or read a good book, or studied at college. If they earned some money that they could spend themselves, they would have more freedom, and more self-respect. Many women liked what Betty Friedan wrote. By the early 1970s, five million copies of her book had been sold worldwide.

American author Betty Friedan (born 1921). Her book The Feminine Mystique *inspired many women to think about what was wrong with their lives.*

A 1950s advertisement for kitchen equipment. Newspapers, TV and other media told women that their place was in the home.

This 1960s housewife from Baltimore, USA, lived in an apartment with no running water. Instead she had to fetch clean water for her family from a tap in the back yard. Like many women, she did not have the luxury of feeling bored.

Jobs at risk

Friedan's book was also greeted with anger. Many men, and some women too, were afraid that the freedom she described would destroy society and wreck the economy. Friedan wrote that if women stopped buying the latest washing machine or vacuum cleaner, many factories would have to close. Many factory-workers would then lose their jobs. If women competed with men for careers, fewer men would have interesting, well-paid jobs. Without stay-at-home wives, men would have to share in boring household tasks.

A different problem

The women Friedan described were certainly miserable, but, in some ways, they were the lucky ones. They had the time and energy to feel bored and depressed. For poor families in Europe and the USA it was not possible for wives to stay at home, even if they wanted to. These women had to find ways of earning extra money for the family. They took part-time jobs, in shops and factories or as cleaners – work that was usually low paid and boring. They had no chance to train for interesting, well-paid careers. Very often, their husbands or families expected them to do all the housework and child care as well. Their problem was exhaustion and poverty, and the lack of any real opportunity to change their lives.

15

THE SECOND WAVE

Equal rights for all

Back in the 1920s the First Wave of organized campaigning by women in Britain and the USA had ended when women won the right to vote on equal terms with men. During the 1960s and 1970s, a Second Wave of campaigning began. It started in the USA, but soon spread throughout Europe.

... in jobs we do full work for half pay, in the home we do unpaid work full time. We are commercially exploited by advertisements, television and the press; legally, we often only have the status of children. We are brought up to feel inadequate, educated to narrower horizons than men...
FROM THE MANIFESTO OF BRITISH WOMEN'S LIBERATION WORKSHOP, 1969

... we whose hands have rocked the cradle are now using our heads to rock the boat ...
WILMA SCOTT HEIDE, 1971

A woman graduate. By the 1970s, there were many well-educated, well-qualified women in America and Europe.

Changing the law

What were Second-Wave women campaigning for? They wanted equal job opportunities and equal pay. They wanted cheap contraceptives and affordable child care. They demanded the right to have an abortion if they chose. They wanted easier divorce, and time off work when they had a baby or their child was ill. They held meetings, lobbied governments, and wrote articles arguing their case.

The US Commission on the Status of Women was led by two female politicians – Eleanor Roosevelt and Esther Peterson (shown here second from the left, next to President Kennedy).

A good start

At first, it looked as if things would change, at least in the USA. In 1961, US President Kennedy agreed to set up a Commission (a committee) to study the status of women. In 1963 the Commission published its report. It found that women were treated unfairly compared with men, in almost every area of American life. It made 24 suggestions for major changes in the law.

Mixed results

In Europe as well as America new laws were passed. They brought improvements, step by step. Most of the advances were made in women's employment rights and women's pay (see pages 30–31). In 1965, positive discrimination was made legal in the USA. This meant that women applying for jobs were chosen rather than men whenever possible. In Britain this was banned.

Easier divorce

In 1969, the state of California introduced the first no-fault divorces. This allowed husbands and wives to agree to end a marriage peacefully. Before that, a wife or husband had to prove that their partner had caused the marriage to break down. That partner lost many rights, including the right to look after the children born during the marriage. No-fault divorce was copied by many other states. British divorce laws were also reformed in the same year. For the first time in Britain, women had equal rights with men to seek a divorce.

Women in 1976 campaigning for the Equal Rights Amendment outside the White House (the home of the US president). Women throughout the USA campaigned for equality.

Constitutional disappointment

Despite all the changes, there was one big disappointment. In 1982, the Equal Rights Amendment, which would have guaranteed equal rights for women, failed to win support from enough US states. It had first been introduced in 1923, and was finally passed by Congress in 1972. But it did not gain enough support from the US states for the amendment to be added to the US Constitution, the most important legal document in the land.

New experiences

Women in the 1960s and 1970s hoped to change more than laws. They wanted to change the way people thought about women, and to introduce new feminist ways of thinking. They also invented new ways of organizing their campaigns.

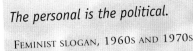
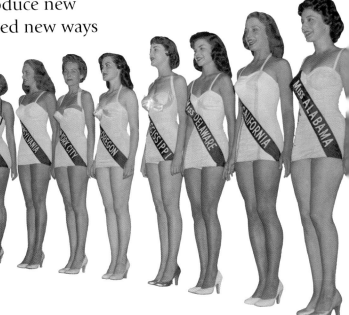

Feminists protested against beauty contests. They argued that women should not be judged by their appearance alone.

Campaigning for women

During the early 1960s, many women had learned how to protest and organize by taking parts in civil rights campaigns (see pages 8–9). They now used this experience to campaign for women's rights. America's National Organization of Women (NOW) was formed in 1966. It was the first of many similar groups in Europe and the USA.

Women's liberation protesters in front of the Statue of Liberty, New York, USA. The phrase 'women's liberation' was first used by a group in Chicago.

EQUAL RIGHTS NOW

INDEPENDENCE NOT DEPENDENC

Direct action

Members of these groups wrote letters and newspaper articles and lobbied politicians. When companies treated women unfairly, they took the companies to court. In 1968, members of New York Radical Women demonstrated outside the Miss America contest in Atlantic City. They argued that beauty contests reduced women to sex objects. They knew that their protest would gain attention for their cause.

Bra-burners?

Outside in the street, they set fire to glamorous clothing. It was reported that they also burned bras, although this was not true. But the idea of feminist bra-burners appealed so strongly to news reporters (and to their readers) that the story was repeated all round the world. In all their protests, women were keen to behave in a peaceful way. They wanted to show that women, unlike men, did not use violence.

WHAT IS A FEMINIST?

Women did not all agree on what a
feminist was. Some saw men as enemies.
Others argued that men were also
trapped by society's rules. Here are three
definitions of feminist used by
campaigning women:

- *A woman who thinks about her own
affairs when men think she ought not to.*
- *Someone who fights
for women as a class...*
- *A person, male or female ... who ...
places the female in the centre
of life and society...*

*Women's liberation demonstrators first marched
through London in 1971. They carried symbols
of women's lives – a washing line, shopping bag
and a dress-designer's dummy.*

Raising consciousness

The most important organizations within
the women's movement were small local
meetings. These discussion groups were
known as consciousness-raising groups.
They were relaxed and friendly and open
to everyone. Consciousness-raising could
mean many things – listening to problems,
suggesting new ways of living, discussing
the latest feminist books, planning
campaigns. It made women realize that they
all had something in common – the fact that
they were women – and that this led to
difficulties in their everyday lives.

Personal or political?

Together, they realized that their own
personal problems were part of a wider,
political issue – the way women were treated
by society. If they felt isolated, humiliated
or unfulfilled, it was because their lives were
ruled by how men expected them to live.
This was summed up in the slogan – 'the
personal is the political'.

*Non-white women were treated
especially unfairly. Coretta
Scott King (speaking), widow
of Martin Luther King, led a
group that demanded
equal rights with whites
and with men.*

THE FEMINIST DEBATE

Women's voices

Women in the 1960s and 1970s wanted women's achievements to be better known and understood. This was an important part of their campaign for equality. They also wanted to change the way that art, history and language usually ignored women's achievements.

> *Women's history is the primary tool for women's emancipation.*
>
> GERDA LERNER (QUOTED IN THE MAGAZINE Ms, 1981)

Simone de Beauvoir was a French feminist. In 1949 she published The Second Sex, *which looked at how men and society treated women.*

Feminist books

Women's writing explored women's feelings and described their lives. For example, Maya Angelou, a black novelist, made a big impression with her autobiography *I know why the caged bird sings*, published in 1970. It described how as a child she suffered poverty and abuse, but it showed courage, hope and humour as well. Germaine Greer, an Australian scholar, shocked many readers with her book *The Female Eunuch*, which criticized men's attitudes to women.

American Gloria Steinem, editor of Ms *magazine, speaking at a news conference in 1977.*

New magazines

Feminist magazines, such as British *Spare Rib* (from 1972) and American *Ms* (from 1971), discussed topics that women felt were important. Instead of household hints and knitting patterns, they had articles on careers and equal pay. Many newspapers also began to include special pages dealing with women's issues.

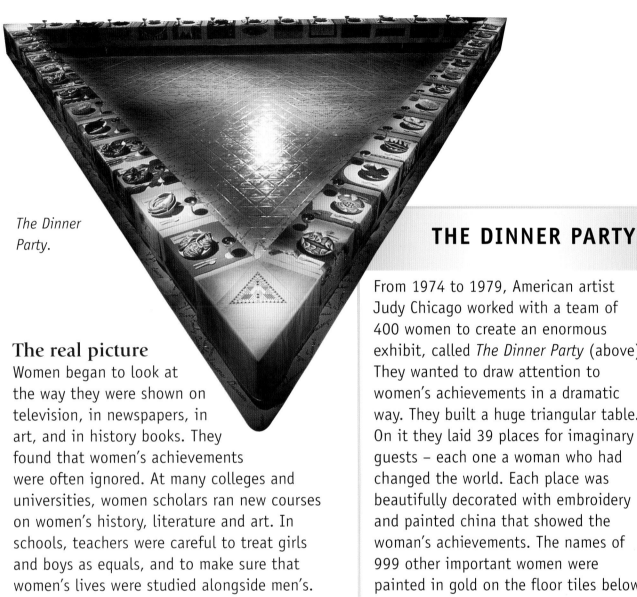

The Dinner Party.

The real picture

Women began to look at the way they were shown on television, in newspapers, in art, and in history books. They found that women's achievements were often ignored. At many colleges and universities, women scholars ran new courses on women's history, literature and art. In schools, teachers were careful to treat girls and boys as equals, and to make sure that women's lives were studied alongside men's.

THE DINNER PARTY

From 1974 to 1979, American artist Judy Chicago worked with a team of 400 women to create an enormous exhibit, called *The Dinner Party* (above). They wanted to draw attention to women's achievements in a dramatic way. They built a huge triangular table. On it they laid 39 places for imaginary guests – each one a woman who had changed the world. Each place was beautifully decorated with embroidery and painted china that showed the woman's achievements. The names of 999 other important women were painted in gold on the floor tiles below.

Germaine Greer in 1975. In her book, The Female Eunuch, she concluded that men must hate women, because they treat them so badly.

Women's words

Until the 1970s, most married women in Europe and America were known by their husband's name. (Miss Mary Jones became, for example, Mrs John Smith.) Feminists did not like this loss of identity, and decided not to change their names when they married. They also protested about the title Mrs, pointing out that men were not given a different title when they married. They used the title Ms instead, which applied to all adult women. Feminists also objected to the way in which words, such as mankind, were used to describe women when neutral words, such as humanity, could be used.

Backlash

Campaigning feminists were only ever a small number of women in the 1960s and 1970s. Many women agreed with feminist ideas, but thought that outspoken feminists sometimes went too far. A few women did not agree with feminist campaigns at all. What were their reasons?

Opposed to change

Some anti-feminist women were influenced by politics. These were women who were usually opposed to all kinds of change. In America, for example, writer Phyllis Schlafly founded the Stop Era (Equal Rights Amendment – see page 17) campaign. She described feminists as dangerous people who wanted to destroy society.

> *The claim that American women are downtrodden and unfairly treated is the fraud of the century.*
> PHYLLIS SCHLAFLY, WRITER QUOTED IN Ms, 1974
>
> *Submission is God's design for women.*
> BEVERLY LaHAYE, CHRISTIAN WRITER, 1976

Phyllis Schlafly campaigned against feminist ideas. Here, she is speaking at a rally against the Equal Rights Amendment.

Arianna Stassinopoulos was a well-known commentator and writer. Here she signs a copy of her book The Female Woman, *published in 1973.*

Anti-American

Schlafly criticized feminists for being scruffy and unfeminine. She claimed that they aimed to destroy the family, and did not want, or care for, children. They were socialists and revolutionaries, and enemies of the state. In fact, they were against the whole American way of life!

Why worry?

Many anti-feminists came from rich families. Their good education and important friends made it easier for them to succeed in a man's world. Unlike ordinary women, they could have families and careers too. In Britain, Arianna Stassinopoulos wrote a book in which she said that feminists ignored women's wishes for love and children. In fact many feminists wanted women to fulfil themselves and be wives and mothers too.

This is part of a newspaper cartoon by Posy Simmonds. It shows the effort needed to be a businesswoman, mother, cook and wife.

In 1975, feminist Shirley Conran wrote a book called Superwoman, *which claimed that women could have a family and a career. Posy Simmonds' cartoon suggests that being Superwoman was not easy.*

A waste of time

Other anti-feminist women came from poorer groups in society. They thought that protesters were wasting time and money that could have been spent on welfare, education and health care for the very poor. What made feminists unhappy, they said, was their unrealistic and unnatural wish to be equal to men.

Against God

Some of the strongest opponents of feminism came from religious organizations. They quoted the Bible and other holy texts, and claimed that God had created woman to be obedient to men.

CHANGING THEIR MINDS

Many women who had strong religious beliefs thought that feminist ideas were wrong. But some became convinced from their own experience, or by talking to other women, that the feminist movement could help women to live better lives. For example, American Sonia Johnson (born 1936), who had a deep religious faith, at first opposed the Equal Rights Amendment (ERA). But she later came to support it and led a march on Washington DC, even though her church expelled her as a result. Johnson used her feminist and religious beliefs to help found the campaigning organization Feminists International for Peace (in 1984).

OUR BODIES, OURSELVES

A woman's choice?

The issues of contraception and abortion caused more distress and anger than any other feminist demand. Many religious leaders and politicians argued that both were wrong. But feminists argued that women had the right to control their own bodies.

Women's bodies

Our bodies, Ourselves was a popular book published in 1969. It explained clearly how women's bodies work. Today, it is difficult to realize how ashamed many women felt about their bodies at that time. Once women understood their bodies and learned about common female diseases, they were able to stay healthier and seek medical treatment earlier. They also felt more in control of their own lives.

The pill

By 1950, contraception was legal in most of Europe and most of America, although only married women could buy it easily. It was expensive, and not very reliable. Then in 1961 the first contraceptive pills were made. These early pills had side-effects and dangers, but compared to earlier methods of contraception, the pill was very reliable. For the first time ever, women could control how many children they had and when.

Many women around the world welcomed the chance to plan their families. Here, a nurse discusses birth control with a group of women in Indonesia.

(Right) People campaigning with posters for and against abortion in Washington, USA, in 1984.

Unwanted pregnancies

Before the contraceptive pill, many women's lives were ruined by unplanned pregnancies. Unmarried mothers were often treated as social outcasts, and few were allowed to keep their babies. They were made to give them up for adoption and many spent years of grief and shame. Unmarried mothers who decided to keep their babies faced poverty and hardship, and often insults as well.

Abortion

Many unmarried pregnant women risked having an illegal abortion. This was very dangerous and thousands of women died each year in Europe and in the USA. To stop this waste of women's lives, feminists (and male doctors and politicians who supported them) campaigned for abortion to be carried out safely and legally in hospital.

MORAL ISSUE

Abortion was made legal in Britain in 1968 and in the USA in 1974. But it was allowed only in special cases, for example to protect the mother's health. Campaigns for legal abortion for everyone caused arguments that still continue today. Many men and women believe that abortion is murder and should never be allowed for religious or moral reasons. Other men and women believe that it is a woman's right to choose whether to have a baby.

In 1972, these men dressed up as pregnant women. They wanted to draw attention to the women's demands for better family planning services in Britain.

In control?

Feminists campaigned for women's right to control their bodies in other ways. They led protests against crimes in which men were violent to women, such as rape and attacks by partners who beat their wives. Feminists also argued for a woman's right to wear whatever clothes she wanted.

Domestic violence

Violence against women was made illegal in 1950. But when some partners were angry, depressed or drunk, they still attacked their wives. Many women found it difficult to escape domestic violence. Often the police would not help. Sometimes the woman was too frightened to complain. If she left her partner, she had nowhere to go and no way of providing for her children.

> Women are entitled to dress attractively ... to be friendly with casual acquaintances and still say no at the end of an evening without being brutally assaulted.
>
> BRITISH (MALE) JUDGE, 1988

A safe place to hide

In 1971, the first refuges for women were opened in Britain and the USA. They gave women and children somewhere to go to escape from violent men. They also provided medical care and legal advice, and helped women to find new homes. Refuges were so badly needed that 250 more were opened in the USA within the next 10 years.

Women and children at Britain's first women's refuge, set up by Erin Pizzey in Chiswick, London, in 1974. Pizzey's campaigns made people realize that violence against women was very common.

Women from many different backgrounds march together in a torchlit procession to protest against violence against women.

Reclaim the Night!

Feminists also campaigned to alter the laws on rape. They marched through areas where women had been attacked after dark, to Reclaim the Night. Some men said that being raped was sometimes the woman's fault. They claimed that, if a woman wore attractive clothes or went out alone, it was her fault if she was attacked. It took years to persuade law-makers, judges and juries that rape was always wrong.

Anything goes

Feminists also demanded that women should be free to dress as they pleased. They felt that it stood for an important right – the freedom to be themselves.

Successful women athletes also influenced fashions. Young women copied their strong, appearance, and brightly coloured, revealing sports clothes.

FEMINIST FASHIONS

Not all feminists dressed in baggy, sensible clothes (see below). Some chose to wear feminine, revealing styles. In the 1960s mini-skirts were popular. From the 1970s onwards, tight-fitting, glamorous clothes were fashionable. When trouser-suits became popular in about 1975, many feminists wore them to rebel against man-made rules. This sometimes led to arguments with employers and others, who thought that women could not look smart in trousers.

Sensible clothes

In the 1970s and early 1980s, many women chose to wear baggy clothes, flat shoes, and no make-up. They wanted to show that being a woman was about more than clothing. Sensible clothes were also more comfortable and practical than fashionable ones. Many feminists said that women should not have to wear high heels and uncomfortable clothes just to look attractive. They should be admired as they were.

WOMEN AT WORK

New careers

In 1976, an American TV executive said that audiences preferred to hear news from a man's voice than from a woman's. People also used words such as lady doctor or authoress, which suggested that these jobs were normally practised by men.

> The world cannot afford the loss of the talents of half its people if we are to solve the many problems which beset us.
>
> Dr Rosalyn S. Yalow,
> Nobel prize-winning scientist, 1977

Education

Gradually, women challenged these views. This was partly through better education. In the 1960s and 1970s more women went to college and university than ever before. From the 1980s onwards, governments encouraged teachers to give girls extra help to study maths and science so that they would have more careers to chose from.

Changing families

Easier divorce (see page 17) and new ideas about family life (see page 40) meant that many more women could have life-long careers. Unlike their mothers, they did not expect a male partner to support them. New ways of working, based on shifts, job-sharing and part-time work, made it easier for women to work, bring up children and run a home. Even so, child care was often a problem. Many feminists demanded free child care for all, but outside Scandinavia and the Netherlands it was rarely available.

New ideas about marriage meant that some fathers stayed at home to look after the children (right) while mothers went out to work.

Earlier in the century few women worked at the top of their professions. There were exceptions, such as Professor Dorothy Hodgkin, who was awarded the Nobel Prize for Chemistry in 1964.

Laws – and good advice

New laws (see box) helped women to follow their chosen careers. Women formed networks, such as Women in Media, to support women working in jobs mostly held by men. Children's books began to show pictures of women doing a wide range of jobs. The American Ms Foundation for Women organized the first Take Our Daughters to Work Day on 28 April 1993. Its aim was to make girls 'visible, valued and heard'.

New opportunities

From the 1960s onwards, new kinds of jobs, in publishing, journalism, television, computing and electronics, opened up for women. Women also worked in fast-growing service industries – for example, as travel guides and air hostesses. There were very few women jet pilots, however, and men still held the most senior jobs.

Young and fashionable women such as 1960s TV personality Cathy McGowan found popular and highly-paid jobs in television and other media.

NEW LAWS

In America, the Civil Rights Act of 1964, stated that all jobs must be equally open to men or women of all races. The Equal Employment Opportunity Commission was set up to make sure the new laws were kept. (It received 50 000 complaints in its first five years.)

In Britain, the Sex Discrimination Act of 1975 made it illegal to treat women differently from men in jobs, housing or education. In the same year, the Employment Protection Act gave women rights to paid maternity leave and to return to their job after their baby was born. At the same time the Equal Opportunities Commission was set up to make sure these laws were kept.

Equal pay, equal chances

More and more women wanted the chance to have well-paid careers, and new laws were passed to give women equal pay for equal work. Yet between 1945 and the year 2000, very few women earned as much as men.

Low pay for women

After 1945 more and more women began to go out to work. By 1960 a third of women in the US worked, and by 1980 more than a half of all women went out to work. But women were never paid as much as men. By 1990 women in the US earned only about two thirds as much as men. In the UK they earned about three quarters.

Pocket-money wages

There were several reasons why women were paid less. Most women still did unskilled jobs. They often worked part-time, and few belonged to unions that would fight for better pay. Men were seen as the family breadwinners and women's pay was thought of as pocket money to add to the family income.

Equal pay at last

Feminists knew that this was not fair. They held strikes and demonstrations to demand better pay. They targeted companies that employed mainly women, such as shops, offices and clothing factories. Governments in Europe and the USA responded by passing laws to improve women's rights to equal employment and equal pay. In America, for example, the Equal Pay Act (1963) made employers give the same wages to men and women who were doing the same jobs.

In 1981 Sandra Day O'Connor was the first woman to become a Supreme Court Justice in America. This was a breakthrough for women in the legal profession.

From the 1980s many women decided to set up their own business, rather than fight to be recognized by male bosses. Anita Roddick set up and ran a very successful chain of shops selling beauty products.

The glass ceiling

By the year 2000, more women than ever before held senior posts, as managers and decision-makers (see box). Some of them were well paid but most women were shut out of the top jobs, and the highest pay, by an invisible barrier called the glass ceiling. Feminists claimed that women were kept out of the top jobs, because men did not trust women or believe in their abilities.

Not ruthless enough

Other people argued that women were not ruthless enough to push rivals out of their way, and that women were not prepared to give their whole lives to their work. They said that part-time work and taking time off to bring up children damaged women's chances of promotion.

WOMEN MANAGERS

The figures below show the percentage of women who worked in management and administrative jobs in different countries in the mid-1990s.

More than 40%:
USA, Canada, Australia

26–40%:
UK, Scandinavia (except Denmark), Italy, Bulgaria, Morocco, Colombia, Botswana, New Zealand, Hungary

10–25%:
Germany, Netherlands, Belgium, Poland, Spain, Mali, much of South America, China, Zimbabwe, South Africa

Less than 10%:
France, former USSR, India, much of Africa, Turkey, Iran

Four Vice-Presidents of the Bank of America sign a business deal with a client in 1984. Two of them are women. By the 1980s, women held top jobs in big corporations.

WOMEN AND POLITICS

Taking part

During the 1960s, many feminists did not want to join any of the main political parties. They disliked their formal rules and the fact that men dominated most political debates. Taking part in politics meant long days travelling away from home, which did not fit in with family life. But soon women realized that they would have to become members of Parliament (in Britain) or of Congress (in the USA), if they really wanted a share of power.

> *You change laws by changing lawmakers.*
> SISSY FARENTHOLD, TEXAS POLITICIAN, 1978

Twice as good

Women discovered that it was difficult to be chosen as a candidate, or to be elected. People said that a woman had to be twice as good as a man to succeed in politics. Men who selected candidates did not think female politicians would be as capable as men. Voters worried whether women were tough enough to represent their views.

Emily's List

In 1971, the National Women's Political Caucus (a committee for choosing political candidates) was founded in the USA by Betty Friedan, a writer, Bella Abzug, a lawyer, and Shirley Chisholm, a former teacher. They encouraged women to put themselves forward for public office. Women from all political parties could belong to it. In 1984, an organization called Emily's List was set up to raise funds to back feminist candidates. In Britain, national conferences during the 1970s encouraged women to try to become elected to government.

A member of the Conservative party in Britain puts up election posters in 1950. At this time most women in politics worked behind the scenes helping male politicians.

Barbara Castle photographed in 1974. She was the minister in charge of social services for the Labour government at the time.

HOW MANY WOMEN?

As women politicians proved how capable they could be, the number of women in politics began to increase. In the United States in 1974, women held 16 (out of about 580) seats in Congress. By 1997 they held 62. In Britain in 1997, women held 120 (out of 651) seats in Parliament. In other parts of the world, women were even more successful in winning votes. In Germany and Scandinavia, 25 to 50 per cent of elected politicians were women. In Canada, Italy, Spain, Austria and Switzerland 15 to 25 per cent of elected politicians were women.

Pioneers

For a long time, only a few women politicians managed to make their voices heard. In Britain Barbara Castle was first elected in 1945. People respected her tough no-nonsense attitude, and her campaigns for worker's rights. In the US, Shirley Chisholm became the first black woman elected to Congress, in 1968. She was honest and independent. People called her unbought and unbossed.

Putting women first

In some countries, political parties drew up lists of women-only candidates, to try and make sure that more women were elected. This was first carried out in Scandinavian countries, where laws already gave women equal rights with men in many areas of their lives. In Norway, for example, from 1975 the Labour Party insisted that 40 per cent of the candidates in any election were women. As a result, one in three members of parliament were female – more than anywhere else in the world.

In 1992 Senator Carol Moseley-Braun became the first black woman elected to the US Senate. She was especially interested in education and opportunities for young people.

33

Women at the top

Most women in politics were ordinary members of parliaments. Very few were government ministers, with the chance to make new policies and decide how taxes should be spent. But from the 1960s onwards, a few women did become heads of government. Most were tough and hard-working. Few called themselves feminists, but many believed that women were more capable than men.

Political families

How did these women come to power? Some were born into political families. Indira Gandhi, the daughter of India's first leader after Independence, was elected Prime Minster of India in 1966. Other women became active in politics after their husbands or fathers died. They felt that it was their duty to continue their husband's or father's work. When Benazir Bhutto's father was murdered by political enemies, she vowed to take his place and became Prime Minister of Pakistan in 1988.

If you want anything done, ask a woman.

MARGARET THATCHER, QUOTED IN *TIME*, 1989

Golda Meir (1898–1978) speaking to the United Nations General Assembly in 1953.

A life in politics

Some women leaders grew up with politics. For example, Golda Meir was interested in Zionist (Israeli nationalist) politics while still a teenager in the USA. She made her fiancé promise to emigrate to Israel before she agreed to marry him. Once there, she joined women's groups and workers' groups, and in 1949 was elected to parliament. She was given ministerial posts, ranging from Social Security to Foreign Affairs. She also represented Israel at the United Nations. She became Prime Minister in 1979, and won respect because she was warm and intelligent but also tough.

Indira Gandhi (1917–1984) spent her whole life in politics. When she was a girl, she helped her father entertain foreign statesmen. In 1966, she became Prime Minister of India in her own right.

Margaret Thatcher waving to supporters as she arrived to take up her new post as Prime Minister of Britain in 1979.

A FEMINIST IN POWER

Gro Harlem Brundtland was the only woman leader who called herself a feminist. She became a member of the Norwegian Labour government in 1974, and Prime Minister in 1981. She was especially interested in the economy, the environment and international development. In 1986, she became Prime Minister for a second time, and led a government that included more women than ever before, in any part of the world. It had eight female ministers and nine male.

A tough approach

Some women were loyal party members. Some had their own ideas. Most were tough, dedicated and hard-working, but few were feminists. They often inspired hatred, as well as admiration. Margaret Thatcher was elected to Parliament in Britain in 1959, as a member of the Conservative party, and became the first woman Prime Minister of Britain in 1979. She was praised and blamed for her many new social policies, and for leading Britain into war against Argentina.

Something must be done

Some women became involved in politics because they felt strongly about one particular issue. For example, Petra Kelly joined the German Social Democratic Party in 1970, but found that it did not share her ecological, feminist views. She started the Green Party in 1979 to protect and preserve the environment. Their ideas spread across Europe. In 1984, Kelly was elected to the West German Parliament. She campaigned against nuclear weapons, and for peace and justice, and women's rights.

Wilma Mankiller (born 1945) became Principal Chief of the Cherokee Native American people in 1985. She was the first woman ever chosen for this honour.

Alternative action

Since the 1960s, women have played an important part in alternative politics. (Alternative means working in new ways, outside the main political parties.) Some women wanted to protect the environment or endangered species. Others tried to ban nuclear weapons, or to bring freedom and justice to people who were badly treated. They all wanted a better, more peaceful world.

Betty Williams (third from left) and Mairead Corrigan (third from right) campaigning for peace in Northern Ireland.

Nuclear bombs – no thanks

Greenham Common Peace Camp was one of the most famous places where women protested. The camp was set up outside a US army base in Britain where nuclear-tipped Cruise missiles were stored. Groups of women lived for years in tents pitched on muddy ground. They said prayers, held vigils and simply asked for peace.

Women protesters holding hands on top of one of the silos where Cruise missiles were stored.

Women for peace

Women also campaigned for peace in Northern Ireland. Here Protestant and Catholic communities were divided by centuries of fear and misunderstanding. Mairead Corrigan (a Catholic) and Betty Williams (a Protestant) led peace marches and encouraged women from both communities to meet each other. In 1975 they won the Nobel Peace Prize.

Saving the planet

Some of the first, and most effective green campaigners were women. An ecologist called Rachel Carson caused a sensation with her book *Silent Spring*, which was published in 1962. It warned people of the dangers of pesticide pollution. Her warnings have since come true. Independent-minded biologists Jane Goodall and Dian Fossey studied and protected apes in different parts of Africa. Both were criticized for their un-scientific approach, but their work has since been appreciated by many people.

Direct action

In the USA, many women continued to campaign for peace and social justice once the civil rights movement (see pages 8 and 9) had ended. For example, Dolores Huerta wanted to improve the conditions of poor Mexican-American farmworkers. She set up peaceful boycotts of grape and lettuce crops, but was beaten and seriously injured by the police. Maggie Kuhn founded the Grey Panther movement to protest against the way elderly people were treated by society.

Reaching hearts and minds

Women in established political parties always had to fit into organizations set up and run by men. But women in alternative politics have been free to invent new ways of taking political action. Most women have protested without using violence. They have written songs and poems or created images that stirred people's ideas and feelings. The women at Greenham Common, for example, pinned baby-clothes onto the razor wire around the camp. These were a symbol of innocence and new life.

RIGOBERTA MENCHU

Menchu was a Quiche Native American who was born in 1959 in Guatemala. She and her father campaigned to stop the ill-treatment of poor farmers by government armies, rich landowners and international big businesses. She went on campaigning even after her father and many members of her family were murdered, and her village was destroyed. In 1987, she set up a committee to try to solve disputes between poor farmers and their attackers by peaceful means. In 1991, she created an international organization to campaign for human rights for Native peoples throughout South America. In 1992, she was awarded the Nobel Peace Prize.

Joan Baez at a peace rally in London in 1965. Like many singers she used words and music to protest against America's part in the Vietnam War.

Struggle for equality

Throughout the twentieth century, women struggled for equality with men. In 1900, women did not have the right to equal education, equal pay or the vote. They relied on their husbands or families for money. Women could not support themselves because their pay was so low. And they were not allowed to enter many careers. Most people believed it was women's duty to care for their family.

> Today, the problem … is how to juggle work, love, home and children …
>
> BETTY FRIEDAN, THE SECOND STAGE, 1981

At last, equal rights!

One hundred years later women's lives had certainly changed. They had the right to vote on equal terms with men. They also had equal rights to education and to training for professional jobs. Governments had passed laws to stop discrimination against women in jobs, wages, housing and in welfare benefits.

A wedding in 1900 (left). Marriage brought security and perhaps happiness, but it limited women's freedom.

No control

Women in 1900 had very little control over their personal lives. There was no safe, cheap contraception. Divorce was very difficult and women could not easily live alone. Make-up and short, revealing clothes were shocking, and not allowed. Women could not play sports in public, or go out to theatres or dances on their own. If a woman lost her respectable reputation, she became an outcast from society.

By the 1990s women were free to behave as they liked. Many stars, such as the singer Madonna, chose to dress and act outrageously, to challenge people's ideas about women.

Norah O'Neill, a cargo pilot, in the cockpit of her jet plane. By the year 2000, women as well as men could have responsible, well-paid careers.

A career – or a struggle to survive?

By the year 2000, many more women worked outside the home in a wide range of careers. Many women found their work interesting, enjoyable and satisfying. They earned enough to live as they chose. But women with children could not always choose whether to work. Some had to work to add to their husband's income, or to support themselves and their children if they had no partner. Many governments encouraged single mothers to return to work, so that the state would not have to give them money.

Working mothers

Most women's work was still poorly paid. Working hours did not often fit in with child care and there were few places at affordable nurseries or playgroups. This meant that it was difficult for working mothers to find someone to look after their children. For women who combined being a mother with a successful career, life could also be very stressful. More women began to suffer from illnesses caused by the long hours and pressures of their work.

Looking perfect

Many women still felt they had to to fit in with an image of beauty shown on television, in women's magazines and in advertisements for make-up and fashion. Most of these companies were owned by men, and many were run by them as well. As well as being good at her job, and a caring, capable wife and mother, a successful woman still had to look perfect as well.

DIVORCE

In 2000 it was easier for a woman to seek a divorce than ever before. Laws in Europe and the USA meant that husbands had to share the family house and belongings with their ex-wives after a divorce. Fathers also had to pay money towards the cost of bringing up their children. This was usually not enough for women and children to live on, because most men did not earn enough to support two households.

By the 1990s, many women had successful careers, and then chose to have a family when they reached their late 30s or early 40s.

The biggest change of all

In the twentieth century, changes in the pattern of family life in Europe and the USA had the biggest effect on women's lives (see box). These changes were brought about by new laws, new ways of working and women's own new ideas.

By the late twentieth century many women were working hard to combine jobs with looking after their homes and children.

NEW FAMILIES

• In 1900, most women lived with their parents until they were married. In 2000, many left their family home at 18 to go to college, or set up home on their own when they started work.

• In 1900, most women married, usually before they were 25. In 2000, many women married later, or did not marry at all. Some lived, unmarried, with a male partner.

• In 1900 it was difficult to get a divorce. In 2000 up to three out of every five marriages in Europe ended in divorce.

• In 1900, it was rare – and shameful – for unmarried women to have children. By the late 1990s in Britain, two out of every five children were born to parents who were not married.

• 1n 1900, most women had children in their 20s or early 30s. In 2000, many women were over 35, or even over 40, when their first baby was born.

• By 2000, many more women lived on their own than in 1945. Young women lived alone before marriage. Divorced and separated women lived apart from their former husbands.

A father with his children in the 1990s. In 1900 a man would not have spent time with his children, sharing cooking or other household tasks.

Important legacy

In the 1980s and 1990s feminism became unfashionable and was attacked by women as well as men. But the affect of feminism has had a lasting affect – in the way it has challenged the roles of men and women in society. It has helped men and women who felt trapped by society to explore new ways of thinking, feeling and living. By the year 2000, it was no longer surprising to see men doing housework, or to find fathers caring for children. By the year 2000 most women agreed that women's lives were better than they had been in 1900. But in many ways, they felt that women were not yet equal with men in society.

A new view of the world

The feminist campaigners of the 1960s and the 1970s hoped to change the way men thought about women and women thought about themselves. They aimed to give women new confidence, with slogans such as 'sisterhood is powerful'. In many ways they succeeded. Their campaigns helped to bring about laws that gave women equal opportunities and equal pay. They also helped to set up and encourage welfare schemes that helped women – such as refuges and rape crisis centres.

Oprah Winfrey (shown on the left) is an award-winning TV star. Her television talk show discusses many issues about women's and men's lives that were first raised by feminist campaigners.

Women pioneers

By 1950, pioneering women had won the right to train for many important careers. They also introduced new and imaginative ways of working, even in big business. Women pioneers also set themselves exciting new challenges in sport, in science and in space exploration.

Arlene Blum (born 1945)

Blum was born in the United States. Although she studied and taught chemistry at university, her real love was climbing. She took part in the first all-woman expedition to reach the top of Denali (or Mount McKinley) in Alaska – the highest mountain in the USA. She organized the American Women's Himalayan Expedition, which successfully climbed Annapurna in 1978. This mountain is the tenth highest in the world and is very dangerous to climb.

Kathleen Lonsdale (1903–1971)

Lonsdale (left) was born in Ireland and became a scientist. She used X-rays to study the way in which chemical molecules are made. She was the first woman to be elected to London's famous Royal Society (an association of top scientists) and was made a Dame. She was a Quaker and was guided throughout her life by her Christian faith. She campaigned for international peace and understanding.

Naomi James (born 1949)

In 1978, New Zealander Naomi James became the first woman to sail on her own round the world. She took just 272 days, breaking the speed record at the same time. She was later made a Dame.

Naomi James

Anita Roddick (born 1943)

Businesswoman Roddick was born in Britain to Italian parents. As a student, she travelled round the world, meeting women and learning traditional health-care and beauty treatments from them. At that time cosmetics companies used many chemicals made in the laboratory. Roddick used the information she had gained on her travels to set up a shop selling cosmetics made with natural ingredients. Soon her Body Shop had grown into a chain of successful shops. She also became involved in environmental and social campaigns and protested strongly against cruelty to animals.

42

*Valentina
Tereshkova*

Clara 'Mother' Hale (1906–1993)

American foster-mother Hale devoted her life to caring for children. Her husband died when she was only 27 years old, and she spent the next 37 years raising 40 foster children. When she was 64 – an age when many women think of retiring – Hale began her fostering career all over again. She realized that some babies needed special care. These babies were born with problems caused, for example, by the fact that their mothers were drug addicts. So she opened a nursery, called Hale House, in New York, where she she cared for 1000 of these babies, including babies born HIV positive. She continued to work for 25 years until she died, aged 87 years.

*Mother Hale with one
of her foster
babies.*

Valentina Tereshkova (born 1937)

Tereshkova won fame in 1963 as the first woman to travel in space. She was born in Russia, the daughter of a tractor driver and factory worker. She became a keen parachutist in her spare time, and volunteered to join the Russian space programme. In 1963, she orbited (flew round) the Earth 49 times. Her space flight was longer than most male space travellers had achieved at that time. Afterwards, she travelled to many countries to speak about her space flight, and became active in Communist politics.

Dame Cicely Saunders (born 1918)

British campaigner Saunders trained as a nurse, doctor and social worker. She is honoured as the pioneer of the hospice movement. Hospices are places where dying people can spend the last months of their lives free from pain and worry, in peaceful, caring surroundings. Saunders raised the money to open her first hospice in 1967 in London. Since then, her ideas have inspired thousands of similar hospices worldwide and have helped millions of dying people.

Women in arts and media

During the second half of the twentieth century, there was an explosion of women's writing and other creative work. Women wrote books, poems and plays to describe their feelings and experiences and to discuss feminist ideas. Women were also successful in new media careers, such as television and film.

Françoise Giroud (born 1916)

Giroud was a French journalist and politician. She was imprisoned by the German army during World War II and after the war become a powerful campaigner for women's rights. In 1945, together with Hèlene Gordon-Lazareff, she founded and wrote for the women's magazine *Elle* (the French word for 'she'). Unlike other publications for women at that time, it combined fashion and beauty with serious discussions on women's place in the world. It brought thousands of readers into contact with the latest feminist ideas. In 1974 Giroud became the first ever Minister for Women in a French government.

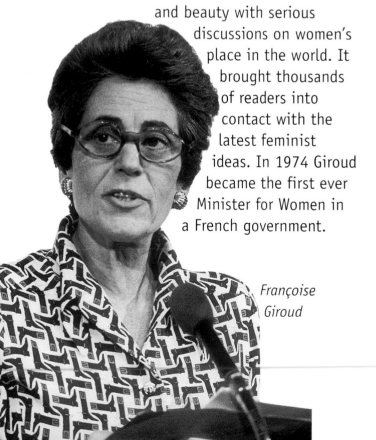

Françoise Giroud

Oodgeroo Noonuccal (1920–1993)

Poet and campaigner Noonuccal was born to Aboriginal and European parents in northern Australia. She was known for much of her life as Kath Walker, but later changed her name to show her Aboriginal background. She left school aged 13, hoping to train as a nurse, but was banned because of racial prejudice. She worked for the Australian Army during the Second World War, then in the 1950s began to write poetry about the Australian landscape and her Aboriginal ancestry. She was one of the leaders of a successful campaign to win equal legal rights for Aboriginals in 1967. In 1970, she was awarded an MBE (a title of honour) by the Australian government, but handed it back in 1988, to protest against 200 years of European-Australian rule.

Ama Ata Aidoo (born 1942)

Born in Ghana, Aidoo taught at a university, and served as a government minister. But she won most fame for her novels and has been called the finest living African woman author. Aidoo's writing is powerful and vivid. Her books describe women's lives in traditional African society, and how they were changed by contact with Europeans.

Maya Lin (born 1960)

Lin was born in Ohio into a family that originally came from East Asia. She trained as an architect and was chosen to design the prestigious Vietnam Veterans' Memorial in Washington DC when she was only 22 years old. Since then, Lin has designed other major works, including a civil rights memorial in Alabama, a sculpture that honours famous women, and a garden made of recycled glass.

Alice Walker (born 1944)

Walker was born into a poor farming family in Georgia, USA, and was the youngest of eight children. She studied at university, became a welfare worker, and then took part in many campaigns for civil rights. In 1968, she wrote about her experiences in her first book, called *Once*. In her most famous work, *The Color Purple*, Walker described the lives of black women who faced prejudice, hardship and violence with great strength and courage. *The Color Purple* won the Pulitzer Prize in 1983. It was also made into a successful film.

Alice Walker

Carmen Callil (born 1938)

Callil was born in Australia to parents whose families had come originally from Ireland and the Lebanon. Callil came to live in Britain in 1960 and worked for several major publishers. Then in 1972, she decided to start her own company. She called it Virago, which means 'strong woman'. It was the first publisher in Britain to produce books written only by women. Virago books soon became well known and successful, and helped to spread many new feminist ideas.

Carmen Callil

Jane Campion (born 1954)

Film-maker Campion works in Australia and New Zealand. After she finished training, she joined the Australian Women's Film Unit. This group helped women to make careers in the Australian film industry, which was controlled by men. Her most famous film, *The Piano*, was made in 1993. It won many prizes and was shown worldwide.

Jane Campion

Oprah Winfrey (born 1954)

Winfrey was born in Mississippi. She began working in local radio while she was still a student at university. By 1985, she had her own morning television show. It covered topics of interest to many women, such as feelings and relationships, in a new and fresh way. Her programme soon attracted one of the largest audiences in the USA. It is now seen in many countries worldwide. Winfrey has also set up her own TV production company. She is a partner in a pioneering venture that links television with the internet. It is designed to appeal especially to young women.

GLOSSARY

boycott A way of protesting. To refuse to have anything to do with somebody or something.

breadwinner The chief money-earner in a family or household.

campaign An organized group of activities, such as speeches or marches, designed to change people's views or win new rights.

career A job with opportunities for progress, training, more responsibility and more pay.

civil rights The rights that allow an ordinary person to play a full part in society, such as the right to vote, receive an education, have a job, marry and follow a religious faith.

Cold War A period of tension between the USA (and its allies) and the USSR (and its allies). It lasted from 1945 to 1989.

communists People who believe in a system of government where there is no private property and no class divisions. Instead, the government owns and runs everything on behalf of the people.

Congress The national law-making assembly of the USA. It is made up of two chambers, the Senate and the House of Representatives.

conservative Wanting to preserve the way things are and opposed to changing them.

constitution The ideas and principles by which a country is governed. Some countries, such as the USA, have a written constitution.

contraception Drugs or devices which prevent a woman from becoming pregnant.

contraceptive pill A pill that prevents a woman from becoming pregnant.

cosmetic surgery Operations, mostly on women, designed to improve their appearance, for example re-shaping the nose or enlarging breasts.

Dame A title that honours great achievements, given by the British Queen on the advice of the government. (The male version is Sir.)

demonstration A public protest.

discrimination Treating people differently because of race, gender, age or religion.

economic Having to do with the management of money.

equality Having the same rights and opportunities, and being treated with respect.

eunuch A man who has had an operation to make him unable to have sex and unable to father children.

extremist Someone who holds very strong views, and who is often prepared to take violent action, or to break the law, to support them.

feminist Someone who believes that women should have the same rights and opportunities as men. Someone who believes that society should be changed to let women achieve equality with men.

fiancé A man engaged to be married to a woman.

green Concerned with the environment and with nature.

international development Links between rich and poor nations designed to help poor nations improve the economy, education and health care.

issue A topic that people feel strongly about.

left wing Having radical, socialist views.

lesbian A woman who is attracted to other women rather than men.

lobbied Tried to make powerful people, such as politicians, change their minds.

militants People with aggressive, outspoken attitudes.

nuclear weapon A weapon powered by the energy given off when tiny particles of matter, called atoms, are split. Nuclear weapons cause massive damage to buildings, and great loss of life.

prejudiced Holding a fixed opinion which is not based on accurate evidence.

racial discrimination Treating people unfairly because of their skin colour or race.

rationed When goods in short supply are shared out in fixed amounts.

razor wire Barbed wire with especially sharp, cutting spikes.

refugee Someone who leaves their homeland to escape from danger.

right-wing Having mostly conservative (see above) political views.

role Originally, the part played by an actor on stage or a film. Also used to mean the part a person plays in government or society.

senator Member of the US Senate (see Congress, above).

service industry A business which offers services to members of the public, such as a shop, cafe, hairdresser, hotel.

side effects Unwanted feelings, like sickness or headache, caused by taking certain drugs.

silo Underground pit.

social services People employed by governments to help disadvantaged people manage their lives, and to help protect vulnerable people, such as children and the elderly, from abuse.

society People living together as a community.

state A separate country ruled by a single government. Belonging to, or organized by, the government of a country.

status A person's rank.

tactics The skill of organizing campaigns.

trade union A group of workers who have joined together to demand better pay and working conditions.

unemployment Being without a job.

welfare benefits Payments made by governments to people who do not have enough money for food, housing, education or health care, or who are unemployed. Also, government-run services, such as hospitals and schools which help the whole community.

White House The official home of the President of the USA.

witch-hunt Seeking out, and unfairly treating, people who hold different ideas or beliefs from most other members of their community.

FURTHER READING
Rees, Rosemary and Maguire, Judith *Living in the 1950s*; *Living in the 1960s*; *Living in the 1970s*; *Living in the 1980s* (Heinemann, 1993)
Thomson, Neil When I was young series: *The Fifties*; *The Sixties*; *The Seventies* (Watts, 1995)
Barber, Nicola *1980s* (Evans, 1993)
Rees, Rosemary; Styles, Sue; Hook, Christa *Britain since 1930* (Heinemann, 1992)
Rowbotham, S *A Century of Women* (Viking, 1997)
Rose, Phyllis *The Penguin Book of Women's Lives* (Penguin, 1995)

INDEX